Introduction

In 2020, as the world shut down, I found myself writing online quizzes for a new group of friends, thinking it would just last until we were all allowed outside again. At the end of the year, I published a few hundred of the questions into a book – *Questioning Your Sanity* – and got ready to call it a day.

But ... why stop then? I was having fun and so, allegedly, were my new friends, while I tortured them with questions about everything from arthropods to zombies. Whether I was getting them to identify famous film quotes from emoji representations, or asking them to recall some of their more obscure chemistry lessons, it remained – and remains – a joy to quiz.

Approaching one hundred quizzes now, I've amassed thousands of questions and so they start earning their keep rather than just sit on my hard drive taking up space, I'm back with a few hundred more brainteasers for you to quiz yourself, your friends, your family or your colleagues. In these pages you will find several dozen rounds that I've tested on people – and a few more that are brand new for this book.

I've tried not to make things too obscure, because it's no fun if you can't even make a guess at them, but if a question seems particularly niche it's probably because I just learnt a bit of scintillating trivia and needed to share it with the world. As an added bonus, I've also peppered the questions with extra facts you can dazzle your players with as and when, because some things are too obscure to be common knowledge, but are too interesting not to share nonetheless. This might be the only book all year that can tell you which Broadway musical used two yak's-worth of hair during its run, who the only non-human member of the Magic Circle is, and when the longest year in history was.

These questions use the novel system of one correct answer being worth one point. Clever, eh? However, there will always be people who want to quibble about how close they got, so I will leave it up to the quizmaster to decide how lenient they want to be. As a general rule, however, I suggest:

- Half a point if the answer is a year and the quizzer is just one year out
- Half a point if the answer requires someone's full name, and only half the name is given

A few questions ask for two answers, to which I offer half a point for each, although you may choose to give a full point for each one.

All the answers are correct at the time of writing. As time moves on, some of them may change, so if in the future you want to argue with an answer, please use whatever the current knowledge suggests. Supplementary research is always welcome, and I daresay even a few of my answers aren't strictly correct, although I've done my best to ensure they are.

The most important thing to remember, however, is just to have fun, because the world always needs a bit more of that. It's been a tricky few years for us all, but spreading a little more fun and knowledge around surely can't be a bad thing. I hope you enjoy these questions and learn a few things along the way too.

Now, grab your pad and pencil and let's get going.

Yours quizzingly,

Michael J Ritchie

@fellfromfiction

Questions

Film & Television

Actors

1. Marlon Brando refused the Best Actor Oscar for which 1972 film?

2. Rex Harrison dedicated his Best Actor Oscar to Audrey Hepburn and Julie Andrews for which film?

3. Which Hollywood actress is credited as having invented an early version of what would become known as Wi-Fi?

4. Name either film that Tom Hanks has, at time of writing, won the Academy Award for Best Actor?

5. In what year did Michael Fassbender, Emma Stone and Andrew Garfield all make their film debuts?

6. Who won Golden Globes for their performances in *Revolutionary Road*, *The Reader* and *Steve Jobs*?

7. Which actress played the wife of a time traveller in 2009, 2011 and 2013?

8. Which superhero is portrayed in film by Jason Momoa?

9. Who played the main role of Beth Harmon in the Netflix series *The Queen's Gambit*?

10. At the 2012 Olympics opening ceremony, which actor played the role of Isambard Kingdom Brunel?

The highest-grossing film performer of all time is Stan Lee, thanks to his Marvel cameos.

Film

1. Who is the eldest of the Von Trapp children in *The Sound of Music*?

2. In the James Bond film of the same name, who is the man with the golden gun?

3. Using the Trojan Horse as inspiration, what large wooden creature do the knights make to break into a castle in *Monty Python and the Holy Grail*?

4. What object does Dumbo have to hold to let him believe he can fly?

5. The final line of which 1969 film is, "Hang on a minute lads, I've got a great idea"?

6. Which film ends with Prince Philip fighting a dragon?

7. Catherine Keener plays the evil Missy Armitage in which 2017 film?

8. In the film *Withnail & I*, what does Uncle Monty wear on his lapel instead of a flower because it has more mystery?

9. Which was the first Pixar film to have humans as the main characters?

10. What word comes before "Western" to describe a sub-genre of film popular in the 60s and 70s that came out of Italy?

Although a lion appears at the start of every MGM film, it has been dubbed over with the roar of a tiger because lion's roars are less impressive.

Reality Television

1. In what year was the first episode of *Made in Chelsea*?

2. Max Morley, Amber Davies and Dani Dyer have all won which reality TV show?

3. Who was the original host of *Streetmate* when it first aired in 1998?

4. In a now infamous episode of *Changing Rooms*, a collection of what were destroyed when the shelves holding them up collapsed?

5. In which Essex town is *The Only Way Is Essex* filmed?

6. Which reality TV series, which began in 2022, was set at Ardross Castle in Scotland?

7. Who is the only presenter to appear on all series of *The Great British Bake Off* as of 2023?

8. Kevin Simm, Leanne Mitchell and Ruti Olajugbagbe have all won which reality TV show?

9. *The Masked Singer* franchise began in which country?

10. What is the name of the companion discussion show for *The Apprentice*?

In 2005, CBS aired a reality television show called The Will, *in which family members and friends competed to be named as a beneficiary in a will. It was cancelled after one episode.*

Science Fiction Films

1. Which science fiction film revolves around the desert planet of Arrakis?

2. What was the home world of Luke Skywalker?

3. What species of creature is the titular alien in the *Alien* films?

4. The film *2001: A Space Odyssey* was based on a short story by which science fiction writer?

5. What was the subtitle of the second *Star Trek* film released in 1982?

6. In the *Back to the Future* trilogy, what is the name of the woman that Doc Brown falls in love with when he travels back to 1885?

7. Who portrayed Dr Ryan Stone in the 2013 film *Gravity*?

8. Which fictional alien attempts to build a device using an umbrella, a coffee can, and a Speak & Spell?

9. Which 1999 comedy film starring Tim Allen and Sigourney Weaver was designed to be a parody of *Star Trek*?

10. Who voiced Buzz Lightyear in the 2022 film *Lightyear*?

Samuel L Jackson asked that his character in Star Wars had a purple lightsaber so he could pick himself out in the battle scenes.

Sitcoms

1. In *Friends*, which soap opera does Joey work on?

2. What is the name of the haunted mansion in the British sitcom *Ghosts*?

3. In *Ted Lasso*, the title character coaches which English football team?

4. Which sitcom features the five main characters Erin, Orla, Clare, Michelle and James?

5. Which Oscar-winner played Sophie Chapman in *Peep Show*?

6. What is the name of Edina Monsoon's daughter in *Absolutely Fabulous*?

7. What was the name of George Mainwaring's unseen wife in *Dad's Army*?

8. Who played Queen Elizabeth I in *Blackadder*?

9. Which sitcom character is often found to be bragging about her exclusive candlelit suppers and her white, slimline telephone with automatic redial?

10. What is the name of the community college in the US sitcom *Community*?

Hugh Laurie and Alan Rickman both auditioned for roles in the sitcom Red Dwarf.

Television

1. Which television series is set in Litchfield Penitentiary?
2. Who won the first series of *Taskmaster*?
3. In *The Simpsons*, what is Marge Simpson's maiden name?
4. Who plays the title character in *The Mandalorian*?
5. In *The Twilight Zone* episode "Time Enough at Last", a bookish man finds himself as the only survivor of a nuclear war, giving him time to read all the books he ever wanted with no interruptions. What fate befalls him just before he picks up the first book?
6. In 2021, who became the fifth host of *Mastermind*?
7. What is the name of the village that Fireman Sam works in?
8. In the 2018 reboot of *Danger Mouse*, who voiced the title character?
9. What was the first thing broadcast in colour on UK television?
10. George was a pink hippopotamus in which children's TV series?

The first advert on Channel 5 was for Chanel No 5.

History

Exploration

1. Which Portuguese explorer was the first European to reach India by sea, doing so in 1498?

2. Who was the first and, so far, only woman to have been on a solo space mission?

3. Hanno the Navigator was a Carthaginian explorer in the fifth century best known for his naval exploration of the coast of which continent?

4. Amy Johnson was the first woman to fly solo from London to which country?

5. What was the name of the first Mars rover to land on the red planet, doing so in 1997?

6. What was the name of the ship that James Cook performed his second and third voyages of exploration of the Pacific?

7. Douglas Mawson, Amyr Klink and Tom Crean are all explorers associated with which continent?

8. In 1925, Percy Fawcett and his team were lost while searching for a lost city known by what single letter?

9. Over which ocean did Amelia Earhart disappear?

10. In what year was the initial release of Internet Explorer?

On his first voyage, Dutch explorer Abel Tasman discovered Tasmania and New Zealand, but entirely missed Australia.

History

1. Sir Francis Walsingham served as the principal secretary and spymaster for which monarch?
2. Tamworth was the capital city of which Anglo-Saxon kingdom?
3. Who was the first emperor of Rome?
4. Who was the last true pharaoh of Egypt?
5. In what year did the Gunpowder Plot take place?
6. In 1921, Albert Einstein won the Nobel Prize in which discipline?
7. Founded in 1788, what was the first permanent city in Australia?
8. What was the dominant political party in the UK between 1715 and 1760?
9. In what year did the *Titanic* sink?
10. On the 23rd March 2021, the Suez Canal was blocked by which ship?

The year 46 BC was actually 445 days long due to the addition of two leap months. It has been nicknamed "the year of confusion", and is the longest year in human history.

Noughties

1. Which city hosted the 2008 Summer Olympic Games?

2. In what year did the first episodes of *The Office, Six Feet Under* and *24* all air?

3. In 2006, Montenegro gained independence from which country?

4. What is the name of the Harvard professor who is the main character in the 2003 novel *The Da Vinci Code* by Dan Brown?

5. Which royal couple married on 9th April 2005?

6. What was the bestselling video game of the 2000s?

7. In which year was Barack Obama sworn in as the President of the United States?

8. Which animated film was the highest grossing film of 2004?

9. In 2009, who was appointed the first female Poet Laureate of the UK?

10. In 2005, the first video was uploaded to YouTube, featuring the site's co-founder Jawed Karim with which animal?

Released in the 2000s, the DVD of Finding Nemo *is the bestselling DVD of all time.*

Prehistory

1. Which historic period lasted approximately from 3300 BCE to 1200 BCE?

2. What natural phenomenon occurred around 75,000 years ago which potentially reduced the human population to around 15,000 individuals?

3. In 2003, fossils of an extinct dwarf species of human were discovered on which island country?

4. Which stone-built Neolithic settlement on Mainland, the largest Orkney island, is sometimes known as the "Scottish Pompeii"?

5. The natural mummy known as Ötzi the Iceman was discovered in which mountain range?

6. In which country have the oldest stone tools outside of Africa been discovered?

7. The Chalolithic period saw a marked increase in the use of which smelted metal?

8. Modern humans evolved from a species called *Australopithecus afarensis*, but what name is given to the first skeleton of this species that was discovered?

9. What is believed to be the first mammal that was domesticated by humans, with evidence dating back 15,000 years ago?

10. The first Neanderthal specimen was found in the Neander Valley in 1856 in which modern-day country?

Ancient Arabic, Hebrew and Chinese languages have no word for "blue". The first society to note the colour were the Egyptians, after they invented a blue dye.

Stuarts

1. Which monarch was the first in the House of Stuart, becoming King of Scotland in 1371?

2. Who was the last Catholic monarch of England, Scotland and Ireland?

3. On which street did the Great Fire of London of 1666 begin?

4. St Paul's Cathedral is built on which small hill in London?

5. Which architect was the first in Britain to employ Vitruvian rules of proportion and symmetry in his buildings, and designed the layout for Covent Garden?

6. In what year was the Act of Settlement, which ensured the succession of the British throne could only be passed to a Protestant?

7. During the English Civil War, what name was given to the supporters of the monarch?

8. During the Interregnum that separated the Stuart era, what title did Oliver Cromwell adopt?

9. During the Glorious Revolution, William III and Mary II arrived in which Devon port town?

10. In 1714, which was the second most populated city in the UK?

In 1710, Native American leaders visited London to meet with Queen Anne. She greeted them personally at St James's Palace, where they were treated as diplomats.

War

1. What was the name of the aerial warfare branch of the German military in World War II?

2. The Battle of Sewell's Point, the Battle of Mount Zion Church, and the Battle of Honey Springs were all part of which war?

3. In which city did Anne Frank and her family hide during World War II?

4. Which king led the English forces in the Battle of Agincourt?

5. Who was the last crowned Anglo-Saxon king of England, losing his throne in the Battle of Hastings?

6. What was the code name during World War II for Germany's plan to invade the USSR?

7. The Boxer Rebellion took place between 1899 and 1901 in which country?

8. Which pole weapon is usually equipped with a vamplate?

9. Which battle took place between 1st July and 18th November 1916?

10. During World War II, Coca Cola stopped being sold in Germany, leading to the invention of which other soft drink that later became the official drink of the Nazi party?

Sidney Lewis is believed to have been the youngest English soldier in World War 1, at just twelve years old. Given you had to be eighteen to join the army, he must have lied very convincingly.

Science & Nature

Animals

1. A silverback is the term given to the group leader of which animal?
2. What is the term for a male rabbit?
3. Which species of bear has a Latin name that literally means "maritime bear"?
4. During which geological period did *Tyrannosaurus rex* live?
5. Which amphibian is the only one to retain gills in its adult form?
6. Which marine invertebrates are found in the class Anthozoa, with a large number of them famously living off the coast of Australia?
7. Which land mammal has the longest tail?
8. Which mammal has species including striped, hooded, and hog-nosed?
9. Farmer Grey, Mr Jeremiah Barker and Squire Gordon all have temporary ownership of which fictional pet?
10. Which American mammal always gives birth to identical quadruplets?

The sea lion is the first non-human mammal proven to be able to keep a musical beat.

Botany

1. Which of these is not a true berry – gooseberry, raspberry, blueberry or watermelon?

2. Which flower appears in the title of a 1957 novel by Ray Bradbury?

3. What plant, associated with Christmas, has the Latin name "ilex"?

4. Allium is the Latin word for what edible plant?

5. What type of plants can be columnar, globular or arborescent?

6. Which flower is sometimes called the "sword lily"?

7. What name is given to the Japanese art of flower arranging?

8. The poison digitalis comes from which kind of flower?

9. The leaves of which tree feature on the logo of the National Trust?

10. What plant tissue transports water and dissolved nutrients upwards from the roots?

Carnivorous plants can count, only snapping shut if they sense two movements in quick succession.

Chemistry

1. Which element is the lightest member of group 15 on the periodic table?

2. As of 2023, what is the last element on the period table, with an atomic number of 118?

3. How many elements on the periodic table are named after historical women?

4. "Mad as a hatter" is a phrase believed to come from men suffering from dementia symptoms due to working with what element used in 19th-century hat manufacturing?

5. Which two subatomic particles are found in the nucleus of an atom?

6. What is the chemical symbol for plutonium?

7. What colour does litmus paper turn under acidic conditions?

8. The elements yttrium, erbium, terbium and ytterbium are all named after a town in which European country?

9. Which element on the periodic table has an atomic number of 3?

10. A tincture of which element, with the atomic number of 53, is used as an antiseptic?

Gold and copper are the only two metallic elements that are not silver or grey in colour.

Creepy Crawlies

1. In The Very Hungry Caterpillar, what does the title character eat on Friday?
2. Which is the largest group of insects – flies, beetles or wasps?
3. What is the name of the ladybird in *A Bug's Life*?
4. What sort of insect would be kept in a formicarium?
5. In the Pokémon games, what sort of insect are the creatures Yanma and Yanmega?
6. Which type of insect sang the song "When You Wish Upon a Star" in a Disney film?
7. What colour is the dye cochineal, which is made from beetles?
8. Which 1904 opera features an insect in the title?
9. What is the term for the anatomical structure used for feeding in place of a tongue by molluscs?
10. In what decade did the VW Beetle first go on sale?

Approximately two thousand silkworm cocoons are required to make one pound of silk.

Dogs

1. What was the name of the first dog in space?

2. What breed of dog's name means "dwarf dog" in Welsh?

3. What was Hong Kong Phooey's day job?

4. In 2000, which band released the song "Who Let the Dogs Out"?

5. The Akita is a breed of dog originating from which country?

6. Which breed of dog has advertised Dulux paint since the 1960s?

7. What is the name of the three-headed dog that guards the Greek Underworld?

8. Which breed of dog is used as a playing piece in Monopoly?

9. Pal was the first dog to play which famous film character?

10. *The Starlight Barking* is the sequel to which novel about dogs?

Dogs are able to remember up to 250 different people and places, and are able to remember events from years before.

Science

1. What is the name of the tubes leading from the ovaries to the uterus?
2. In 1954, Joseph Murray performed the first organ transplant, but what organ was transplanted?
3. In a typical plug socket, what colour is the neutral wire?
4. By what name is dilute acetic acid better known?
5. What is the lowest layer of the Earth's atmosphere?
6. What does the "B" stand for in USB?
7. What is the name of the first human to have been born after conception by IVF?
8. What body part lends its name to the very centre of a storm?
9. What two elements are mixed to make the alloy electrum?
10. What is oology the study of?

Although we absolutely stress that you shouldn't try this at home, scientists have discovered that human stomach acid is so potent, it can dissolve razor blades in two hours.

Space

1. The moons of which planet are all named after characters in Shakespeare plays, including Ariel, Miranda and Puck?
2. Which was the first space mission to land a man on the moon?
3. What did NASA confirm about the moon on October 26th, 2020?
4. Which of Mars's two moons is the largest?
5. The axis of which planet in our solar system has the smallest tilt?
6. Polaris, or the Pole Star, is part of which constellation?
7. What metal present in the surface of Mars gives it its reddish colour?
8. In 1979, Voyager 2 became the first and, so far only, spacecraft to visit which planet?
9. What is found on the moon and measures thirteen by six inches?
10. Pluto is often considered to be a binary system with which of its five moons?

Neptune was discovered in 1846 and didn't complete a full orbit of the Sun until 2011.

People

Daniel(le)

1. Which Daniel played the beat poet Allen Ginsberg in the 2013 film *Kill Your Darlings*?

2. Singer Dannii Minogue served as a judge on which UK talent show from 2007 until 2010?

3. In which James Bond film did Daniel Craig first play the role?

4. Behind Agatha Christie and Barbara Cartland, who is the third bestselling novelist of all time?

5. Although Daniel Kaluuya has appeared in many popular films, and won an Oscar for his role in *Judas and the Black Messiah*, he first rose to prominence in which television series, first aired in 2007, where he played Posh Kenneth?

6. Daniel Day-Lewis, famous for method acting, has now retired but what was his last film, released in 2017?

7. Dani Harmer has played which literary character on television since 2002?

8. Danny Elfman came to prominence as the lead singer and primary songwriter for which new wave band of the 1980s?

9. Name either name that Danielle Moonstar has gone by as a member of the X-Men?

10. Which President did Dan Quayle serve as Vice President for?

Daniel Craig is the first actor to play James Bond who was born after the start of the film series.

George

1. Prior to directing *Star Wars*, how many other films had George Lucas already directed?

2. Which of the Georges is the most recent monarch to be born outside of Great Britain?

3. The monkey Curious George was brought home from Africa by a man wearing what colour hat?

4. What was the name of the doctor George Clooney played in ER?

5. In *Harry Potter and the Deathly Hallows*, what body part does George Weasley lose after a duel?

6. Which George wrote an essay in 1946 entitled "A Nice Cup of Tea", which detailed how best to make tea?

7. What does the W stand for in George W Bush?

8. How many *Star Trek* films did George Takei appear in as Sulu?

9. What was George Michael's first solo single?

10. George Costanza is a main character in which American sitcom?

After Manchester United, the first team George Best played for was Jewish Guild in South Africa, a club that now plays lawn bowling.

Jo & Joe

1. From 1973 to 2009, Joe Biden served as the senator to which state?

2. Joanna Lumley played which character in The New Avengers from 1976 to 1977?

3. In the 1990 film *Joe Versus the Volcano*, who plays the Joe of the title?

4. Joan of Arc appears as a character in which Shakespeare play?

5. Actress Josephine Baker aided which organisation during World War II?

6. Johannes Radebe was teamed up with who to form the first male same-sex pairing in the history of the UK version of *Strictly Come Dancing*?

7. Joanne was the fifth studio album of which artist, released in 2016?

8. Joe DiMaggio played for which baseball team from 1936-1942, and again from 1946-1951?

9. Jo Frost is a British television presenter better known by what nickname?

10. Who succeeded Joseph Stalin as the leader of the Soviet Union in 1953?

In April 2020, it was reported that Joe Biden's presidential campaign had spent $10,000 on ice cream as gifts to campaign donors. Biden acknowledges that ice cream is his greatest vice.

Mary

1.   What was the maiden name of First Lady Mary Lincoln?

2.   What was the title of the 1826 science fiction novel by Mary Shelley, featuring characters including Lionel Verney and Lord Raymond?

3.   In which decade did social activist Mary Whitehouse found the National Viewers' and Listeners' Association?

4.   Which musical Mary has released fragrances called My Life and My Life Blossom?

5.   In the first verse of the nursery rhyme "Mary Had a Little Lamb", where does the lamb follow Mary to?

6.   Which street do the Banks family live on in the *Mary Poppins* books and films?

7.   Which archangel told the Virgin Mary that she was going to be the mother of the Messiah?

8.   Mary Berry claims that she will test an oven she's never used before by baking what cake in it?

9.   Which UK Prime Minister had the first name Mary, although it was not the name she went by?

10. Mary Seacole served as a nurse during which conflict?

Although most women in the Bible are described in relation to the men in their lives, Mary Magdelene is named twelve times, and never with any attachment to a spouse, parent or child.

Michael

1. "Man in the Mirror", "Dirty Diana" and "Smooth Criminal" were all songs on which Michael Jackson album?

2. Michael Fassbender played which businessman in a 2015 biopic?

3. Michael Owen played for which football team from 1996 – 2004?

4. Name either of the two films that Michael Cera starred in that were released in 2007?

5. What was the name of the comedy show that Michael Palin devised with Terry Jones following their work with *Monty Python*?

6. In which 1987 film did Michael Douglas play the role of Gordon Gekko?

7. Michael Scott was the American equivalent of which British sitcom character in the remake of *The Office*?

8. Which Michael of the sports world is sometimes known as the Baltimore Bullet or Flying Fish?

9. What year did Michael Bublé release his self-titled debut album?

10. In Western Christian tradition, on what date is Michaelmas celebrated?

Had Michael Jordan's career in basketball not taken off, he planned to become a weatherman.

Rachel

1. Rachel Stevens was formerly a member of which 2000s pop band?
2. Rachel Riley studied mathematics at which university?
3. Who wrote the 1951 novel *My Cousin Rachel*?
4. In the TV show *Friends*, how many sisters does Rachel have?
5. In the Bible, Rachel was married to which patriarch, sometimes known as Israel?
6. Rachel Mason was the headmistress of which fictional school in a BBC drama of the same name?
7. Rachel Hunter was married to which musician from 1990 to 2006?
8. Which Rachel won the Best Supporting Actress Oscar in 2006 for her role in *The Constant Gardener*?
9. Which Rachel is the first openly lesbian anchor to host a major prime-time news program in the United States?
10. Who played the character of Rachel Zane in the American TV series *Suits*?

England footballer Rachel Yankey pretended to be a boy as a child so she could play in a boy's football team. No one realised she was a girl for two years.

Music & Theatre

Classical

1. *Zadok the Priest* was composed for which monarch's coronation, and has been used in every British coronation ceremony since?

2. Which instrument is the smallest woodwind, and also plays the highest note in an orchestra?

3. What is the first name of the composer Beethoven?

4. The Bayreuth Festival is dedicated to the works of which German composer?

5. Clara Schumann was most famous for playing what instrument?

6. Which planet appears in the name of Mozart's final symphony?

7. Who composed "Clair de lune", which is part of a larger suite?

8. Igor Stravinsky's opera *The Rake's Progress* was based on the paintings of which artist?

9. Which composer, wrote the *Minute Waltz*, now famous for being the theme music for the radio game show *Just a Minute*?

10. What was the nationality of Antonio Vivaldi?

Frederic Chopin's heart is preserved in cognac and kept in a church in Warsaw.

Music

1. Which band released albums including "Zenyatta Mondatta" and "Ghost in the Machine"?

2. Who collaborated with Queen for the 1981 song "Under Pressure"?

3. What was the name of the 2014 album from U2 that was automatically – and controversially – downloaded onto everyone's iPod?

4. Benjamin Balance-Drew is an English rapper better known by what stage name?

5. Bebop, acid, swing and stride are all subgenres of which kind of music?

6. Eleanora Fagan was the real name of which jazz icon?

7. What was the name of Bill Haley's backing group?

8. Which artist was known as the Godmother of Rock and Roll?

9. Which American blues guitarist allegedly sold his soul to the devil in exchange for his career?

10. In *The Muppets*, what instrument did Animal play?

In "Bohemian Rhapsody", Freddie Mercury plays on the very same piano that Paul McCartney played on "Hey Jude".

Musicals

1. Which British musical has the finale song "Tell Me It's Not True"?

2. Which West End musical became a film in 2008 featuring Meryl Streep, Christine Baranski and Pierce Brosnan?

3. Who wrote the music and lyrics for the 1949 musical *South Pacific*?

4. The musical *Rent* is based on which 1896 opera?

5. Which musical contains the "Elephant Love Medley"?

6. Which 2006 musical retells the Greek myth of Orpheus's journey into the underworld to rescue his lover Eurydice?

7. According to the novel and the musical *Wicked*, what is the true name of the Wicked Witch of the West?

8. Which song from the movie *Encanto* became the first song from a Disney film to reach number one in the UK charts?

9. What is the lowest female voice category in opera?

10. "Opening Night" is a song from which Mel Brooks musical?

During its Broadway run from 1981 to 2000, the musical Cats *used 3,247 pounds of yak hair to make the costumes.*

Number Ones

1. What was ABBA's first number one in the UK?

2. The charts began in 1952, with which song being the first UK number one, as well as the first Christmas number one?

3. Which band had the most UK number ones in the 2000s, claiming the top spot 11 times?

4. Which single spent the most consecutive time at the UK number one spot, at sixteen weeks?

5. In the 1980s, which artist spent the most time at number one?

6. The theme song for which James Bond film became the UK number one on 27th February 2020?

7. In 2007, how many weeks was "Umbrella" by Rihanna at number one?

8. "Long Haired Lover from Liverpool" was a Christmas number one in 1972 for which artist?

9. How many number one singles did Amy Winehouse have in the UK during her life?

10. Which member of the Beatles had the most successful song of 1971, holding the number one spot for five weeks?

Kate Bush currently holds the record for the longest time span between number one singles for a female artist. Her first number one, "Wuthering Heights", was released in 1978. Her second was "Running Up That Hill" in 2022.

Theatre

1. Iago is the sinister villain in which Shakespeare play?

2. Which of the first four US Presidents is the only one not to appear on-stage in *Hamilton*?

3. For whom are the Tony Awards named?

4. In which decade did Agatha Christie's *The Mousetrap* begin its record-breaking run?

5. Who wrote the plays *Edward II* and *The Massacre at Paris*?

6. What links the 1970 play *Gandhi*, the 1983 musical *Dance a Little Closer*, and the 1979 revue *Break a Leg*?

7. According to theatre superstition, it is bad luck to bring the feather of what bird onto a stage?

8. Which English playwright won the Nobel Prize for Literature in 2005?

9. Which 2023 musical is about a military operation during World War II and includes the songs "Dear Bill" and "Born to Lead"?

10. What creature does Nick Bottom get turned into in *A Midsummer Night's Dream*?

Choreographer Bob Fosse was the first person to win an Emmy, Oscar and Tony in the same year, doing so in 1973.

Art & Literature

Art

1. Who painted the Sistine Chapel ceiling?

2. The Chandos portrait is a famous painting said to be of which historical figure?

3. Who painted the portrait *Girl with a Pearl Earring*?

4. Which artist is responsible for the work *Self*, first exhibited in 1991, which is a self-portrait formed of ten litres of frozen blood from the artist themselves, and is recast every five years with fresh blood?

5. Chinese artist Ai Weiwei installed an artwork in the Tate Modern in 2010 that consisted of one hundred million individually hand-crafted porcelain what?

6. Which 1942 painting features a restaurant inspired by one on Greenwich Avenue, Manhattan?

7. Which artist used the landscape of New Mexico for her paintings, including *Summer Days* and *Cow's Skull: Red, White and Blue*?

8. Tracey Emin was shortlisted for the 1999 Turner Prize with a work that featured what item of furniture?

9. What is the name of Grayson Perry's female alter-ego?

10. Which artist appears in the painting *Self-Portrait with Monkey*?

The Louvre has a specific letterbox for Mona Lisa because she receives so many offerings, including love letters, flowers and poems.

Books

1. Jonathan Harker is a solicitor in which classic novel?

2. Who wrote the 2018 novel *The Seven Deaths of Evelyn Hardcastle*?

3. *Under the Red, White and Blue* was the originally proposed title for which novel?

4. *One Hundred Years of Solitude* was originally published in which language?

5. Who serves as the detective in the 1941 crime novel *Evil Under the Sun*?

6. According to the opening line of *Mrs Dalloway*, what has the title character decided to buy herself?

7. Charles Pooter is the narrator of which 1892 novel?

8. *Bridget Jones's Diary* is loosely based on which classic novel?

9. Which classic children's tale is the world's most translated non-religious book?

10. Which novel has the opening line, "The snow in the mountains was melting and Bunny had been dead for several weeks before we came to understand the gravity of our situation"?

The most expensive book in the world is the Codex Leicester, a notebook filled by Leonardo Da Vinci. It was purchased by Bill Gates for $30.8 million dollars.

Kids Books

1. What is the surname of the title child in Roald Dahl's novel *Matilda*?

2. Which US state is Dorothy Gale from?

3. Name either of the title character's horrible aunts in *James and the Giant Peach*?

4. What is the name of the town that the Grinch steals Christmas from?

5. In *The Jungle Book*, what kind of animal is Rikki-Tikki-Tavi?

6. Who wrote and illustrated the picture books *Elmer* and *Not Now Bernard*?

7. In the Mr Men series, what shape is shared by Mr Cool and Mr Rush?

8. In the Narnia stories, what is the actual name of the White Witch?

9. In Beatrix Potter's stories, what sort of animal is Mrs Tiggy-Winkle?

10. What is the name of the forest where Winnie the Pooh lives?

The Latin translation of Winnie the Pooh *(*Winnie Ille Pu*) is the only book in Latin to have made the New York Times Bestseller List.*

Literature

1.   What is the name of the university in Ankh-Morpork in the *Discworld* novels?

2.   Which 2009 novel by David Nicholls takes place on multiple St Swithin's Day?

3.   What word links the titles of an 1897 novel by H G Wells and an 1869 novel by Leo Tolstoy?

4.   In which classic novel did a woman sell her chestnut hair for $25 to raise money for her ill father?

5.   Which Charles Dickens character has never recovered from being jilted at the altar and has refused to take off her wedding dress ever since?

6.   In *Brave New World*, what is the name of the drug that keeps citizens happy and compliant?

7.   A 1970 novella by Richard Bach explores the world from the point of view of a bird called Jonathan, but what kind of bird was he?

8.   Which novel features the house Thrushcross Grange?

9.   Who wrote the 2003 novel *The Kite Runner*?

10. What was the first James Bond novel written by Ian Fleming?

If you publish a book in Norway and it passes quality control, the government will purchase a thousand copies. If it's a children's book, they'll buy 1,500 of them and distribute them to libraries across the country.

Statues & Sculptures

1. A bronze statue of which fictional character stands in Kensington Gardens in London, and was unveiled under cover of darkness by the author?

2. The tallest statue in the world is 182 metres tall, but in which country is it found?

3. Which engineer is responsible for the metal framework of the Statue of Liberty?

4. The 1993 statue *Partners* appears in five locations around the world, and depicts which two figures?

5. What material is Rodin's *The Thinker* made of?

6. The artworks *Gift Horse*, *Antelope* and *Really Good* have all appeared in which location?

7. Who designed the *Angel of the North*?

8. As of 2023, who is the only woman commemorated with a statue in London's Parliament Square?

9. Michelangelo's *David* is found in which Italian city?

10. A statue of which fairy tale character can be found off the coast of Copenhagen?

Michelangelo's David *is cross-eyed so he looks perfect from multiple angles.*

Religion & Politics

Judaism

1. At the end of a Jewish wedding ceremony, what does the groom break underfoot?

2. Although Eve is often considered the first woman in the Abrahamic faiths, some debate in Judaism gives this position to which other woman?

3. Many synagogues contain an elaborate chair named for which prophet, which is only sat upon during the ceremony of Brit milah?

4. Which Jewish holiday commemorates the Exodus from Egypt?

5. Around 75% of the world's Jewish population are of which denomination?

6. How many candles are there on a Hanukkah menorah?

7. In the Jewish calendar, what is the first month of the ecclesiastical year?

8. The Torah is made up of the first five books of which collection of ancient Hebrew scriptures?

9. In Orthodox communities, at what age to Jewish girls traditionally have their *bat mitzvah*?

10. Which British sitcom centres around a Jewish family gathering together for a weekly meal?

Fish and chips became a British staple after it was introduced by Portuguese Jews. The first chip shop was opened in 1860 by a Jewish cook, Joseph Malin.

Kings & Queens

1. Which English king was known as the Merry Monarch?

2. Who was the last English king to die in battle?

3. Who ascended to the throne of their country at six months old in 1542?

4. Which flag is flown above Buckingham Palace to denote that the monarch is in residence?

5. Which English monarch reigned from 1547 to 1553?

6. Who became the King of Spain in 2014?

7. Both Elizabeth I and Elizabeth II ascended to the throne at the same age – what age were they?

8. In what year did Queen Victoria die?

9. Who was the last monarch to rule France?

10. Which fictional character appeared alongside Queen Elizabeth II in 2012 to celebrate the opening of the Olympic Games?

When the mummy of Ramesses II was flown to Paris for examination, he was issued a passport that listed his occupation as "King (deceased)".

Mythology

1. Which Egyptian goddess of fertility, children, art and protection had the head of a cat?

2. In Greek mythology, what is the term for the food and drink of the Gods?

3. According to Viking myth, what event serves as the immediate prelude to the events of Ragnarök?

4. Who was the Roman god of thunder?

5. In Christian mythology, how many humans were said to be on Noah's Ark?

6. The Egyptian god Khonsu, Chinese god Jie Lin, and the Hindu god Chandra are all associated with what?

7. In Greek mythology, what is the name of the ferryman on the River Styx who serves as psychopomp?

8. In English, how many days of the week are named after gods?

9. According to Egyptian mythology, after one died, their heart was weighed against what item?

10. In Greek mythology, what is the name of the personification of nothingness from which all existence sprang, usually depicted as a void?

In Norse mythology, the Sæhrímnir is a creature that is killed and eaten every night by those in Valhalla. It is brought back to life the next day to provide sustenance again.

Politics

1. Who is the only British Prime Minister to have been assassinated?

2. Who served as the Taoiseach of Ireland from 2011 to 2017?

3. What name was given to members of the communist party in Cambodia in the 1970s?

4. How long does Prime Minister's Questions last?

5. The Labour Party is traditionally represented by what flower in its logo?

6. Who rules in a kakistocracy?

7. Which UK Prime Minister specified he would be "tough on crime, tough on the causes of crime"?

8. Who served as the Speaker of the House of Commons from 1992 to 2000?

9. Who was the leader of the Liberal Democrats from 1988 to 1999?

10. John Prescott punched a protestor in 2001 after what was thrown at him?

The door to 10 Downing Street cannot be opened from the outside, has no keyhole or functional letterbox, uses a wonky O instead of a 0, and is bombproof.

Religion

1. In Sikhism, what is the name of the dagger worn in a belt at all times?

2. Which month in the Islamic calendar is observed with a month of fasting?

3. Which religion believes that only 144,000 people will ascend to heaven, with everyone else being resurrected after Armageddon?

4. The Panchang is a calendar of which world religion?

5. How many Noble Truths are there in Buddhism?

6. In Christianity, who was the first human that God allowed to eat animals?

7. Which of these countries is not mentioned in the Bible – India, Cyprus or Greece?

8. Shahadah, Salat, Hajj, Sawm and Zakat are the "Five Pillars" central to which religion?

9. In medieval Christianity, what bird became associated with the Passion of Jesus as it was thought to be so attentive to its young that it would wound its own breast to provide the chicks with blood when no other food was available?

10. Which German town is said to have seen Martin Luther nail his 95 theses to a church door?

Although Wicca is frequently considered to be an ancient religion, it only dates back to the 1950s.

World Leaders

1. Who is the only US President to serve more than two terms?

2. What is the minimum age one must be to be eligible for presidency of the USA?

3. Who served as Pope during World War II?

4. The Blue House served as the presidential residence for which country from 1948 until 2022?

5. Augusto Pinochet ruled which South American country from 1974 to 1990 as dictator?

6. Which US President was so unwell towards the end of his presidency that his wife took over and managed the role?

7. Jair Bolsonaro was sworn in as president of which South American country in January 2019?

8. Bill English, Helen Clark and Robert Muldoon have all served as Prime Minister of which country?

9. By what title is Tenzin Gyatso better known?

10. After resigning from office due to the Watergate scandal, Richard Nixon was later pardoned by which US president?

Spy Magazine once sent some of the world's richest people cheques for thirteen cents to see who would cash them. Donald Trump was one of only two people to do so.

Geography

Asia

1. Which Asian country is the fourth most populated nation in the world?

2. What is the largest religion of Sri Lanka, practiced by 70% of the population?

3. In which Asian country is the temple complex Angkor Wat?

4. In what year did the handover of Hong Kong occur, ending British rule?

5. Which country has produced the most Nobel laureates per capita in Asia?

6. What is Asia's largest landlocked country?

7. What is the national fruit of India?

8. What is the national language of Pakistan?

9. Which major river starts in Tibet and ends in the South China Sea?

10. Which Asian city hosted the 1988 Summer Olympics?

China produces 45 billion pairs of chopsticks each year.

Britain

1. In what year did the Aberfan disaster occur?
2. What is the only settlement in England that has a name ending in an exclamation mark?
3. The coat of arms of which UK city contains symbolism regarding the life of St Mungo, including a shield flanked by two fish?
4. The Lake District is entirely within the borders of which English county?
5. Cardiff is the county town of which Welsh county?
6. Three cities in the UK begin with "St.", but which is also the smallest city in the UK by population?
7. Which mountain range is sometimes known as the backbone of England?
8. What is the most common street name in Great Britain?
9. Which river forms most of the border between Devon and Cornwall?
10. On the London Underground, the Waterloo & City line contains only two stations; Waterloo and which other?

When the tide is in, the Isle of Wight is Britain's smallest county. When the tide is out, it's Rutland.

Europe

1. On what peninsula do Spain and Portugal lie?

2. What is the second largest city of Norway by population?

3. Between 1949 and 1990, what city served as the capital of West Germany?

4. Which European country is officially known as the Hellenic Republic?

5. Alphabetically, what is the last member of the EU?

6. Who assassinated Archduke Franz Ferdinand in an event that would lead to the beginning of World War I?

7. What is the second largest theistic religion in Europe?

8. In what year did the band Europe have a UK number one with "The Final Countdown"?

9. What is the capital city of Portugal?

10. In what year did the Easter Rising take place in Ireland, which saw Ireland proclaim independence from the UK?

If you wanted to see every piece of art in the Louvre and spent thirty seconds on each one, it would take about thirty-five days.

Geography

1. What is the world's tallest uninterrupted waterfall?

2. Split is the second largest city in which country?

3. In geology, what is the term for the hollow that forms after the emptying of a magma chamber following a volcanic eruption?

4. What is the southernmost capital city in the world?

5. The longest international border in the world is between which two countries?

6. In which country is the city of Timbuktu?

7. Which US state is known as the Land of 10,000 Lakes?

8. What is the highest level of the rainforest?

9. Which is the only country in Europe to end in the letter G?

10. In which sea is Saint Lucia?

France, Spain and Morocco are the only three countries that border both the Atlantic Ocean and the Mediterranean Sea.

Landmarks

1. The Sultan Ahmed Mosque in Istanbul is sometimes known as a mosque of what colour?

2. What is the tallest free-standing structure on land in the Western Hemisphere?

3. In 1960, Paul Robeson became the first person to perform at which musical venue, singing at "Ol' Man River" to construction workers as they ate lunch?

4. Which London landmark has a lean that is one sixteenth that of the famous tower in Pisa, but isn't likely to be a problem until the year 6000?

5. In which Russian city would you find Saint Basil's Cathedral?

6. The Manneken Pis is found in which European capital city?

7. By surface area, what is the largest loch in Scotland?

8. Which landmark is located on Salisbury Plain?

9. In 1754, William Stukeley said what manmade structure was visible from the Moon?

10. In which country is Machu Picchu?

When the Sagrada Familia is completed, it will have taken longer to build than the Great Pyramids.

Mountains

1. Denali, the highest mountain peak in North America, was known by what other name from 1917 to 2015?

2. The borders of which two countries run across the summit of Mount Everest?

3. Which of England, Scotland, Wales and Ireland has the lowest highest peak?

4. In which American state is Mount Rushmore?

5. What is the name of the mountain that features in Harry McClintock's 1928 song, which tells of a hobo's idea of paradise?

6. The Greek gods lived at the top of which mountain?

7. What is the highest mountain range outside of Asia?

8. In *The Lord of the Rings*, which mountain serves as the endpoint of Frodo's journey?

9. What is the tallest mountain in the Alps?

10. English mountaineer Edward Whymper achieved the first ascent of which European mountain?

There's a mountain in Australia called Mount Disappointment, which was named because the first explorers who first reached its summit were unimpressed by the view.

Sport & Games

Athletics

1. In which athletics throwing event is the women's world record further than the men's?

2. Who was the first black British woman to become an Olympic champion?

3. The Ancient Greek pentathlon featured discus throw, javelin throw, a short foot race, the long jump and which other event?

4. How many times did Paula Radcliffe win the London Marathon?

5. In open competitions, what is the weight of a men's shotput in pounds?

6. In which European city were the 2023 World Athletics Championship held?

7. Which British Paralympian has won 11 gold medals at the Paralympics, and has held over thirty world records?

8. Who achieved fame in 1984, at the age of 17, by unofficially breaking the 5000 metres world record?

9. What is usually the first event in a decathlon?

10. In which athletic event would you find techniques called Scissors, Western Roll and Straddle?

Humans can outrun elephants, pigs and squirrels, but can be beaten by cats, rabbits and kangaroos.

Board Games

1. In the original version of Monopoly in 1935, the streets were based on those of which city?

2. In which language are you playing Scrabble if there are 15 E's, 9 A's and just one W which is worth ten points?

3. In Battleships, what is the largest type of ship that needs to be found?

4. In Trivial Pursuit, what colour is associated with History questions?

5. In the board game Buckaroo, what is the name of the mule?

6. In chess, the act of castling occurs between a rook and which other piece?

7. How many blocks are there in a complete Jenga set?

8. What is the highest number of pips on one end of a standard domino?

9. What colour is the playing piece in Cluedo that represents a character with an academic title?

10. How many dice are used in a traditional game of Yahtzee?

During World War II, Allied prisoners of war were allowed to play board games. The British government sent games of Monopoly that included real money, silk maps, and compasses and files hidden inside the boards. They successfully allowed many soldiers to escape.

Football & Rugby

1. Which Premier League football team was founded under the name Dial Square?

2. How many players are there on a rugby league team?

3. In which UK city is Murrayfield Stadium?

4. In 1974, Brian Clough became manager of Leeds United, leaving which club?

5. Jack Charlton served as the manager for which national football team from 1986 – 1996?

6. Which member of a rugby team is usually the heaviest, and can be either a loosehead or a tighthead?

7. The Springboks are the national rugby union team of which country?

8. Which country won the first World Cup held in 1930?

9. Norwich City FC are known by which avian nickname?

10. A scrum half will traditionally wear what number on their shirt?

The only football team to ever win the World Cup while wearing red were England in 1966.

Sport

1. The first modern Olympics were held in 1896, but in which city?

2. Whose ear did Mike Tyson famously bite in a 1997 fight?

3. Magic Johnson spent his entire career with which basketball team?

4. Which nation hosted the 2023 Cricket World Cup?

5. In Europe, what colour is the top belt in judo?

6. Mark Calaway is a wrestler better known by what ring name?

7. In tennis, what city is the Australian Open played in?

8. In Formula One, what number appears on a pink flag that is waved to indicate there is to be no overtaking?

9. In snooker, how many points is the green ball worth?

10. If your balls are black and blue, and your opponents' balls are red and yellow, what's the game?

The longest tennis match in history took place in 2010 during Wimbledon. John Isner and Nicolas Mahut played for eleven hours and five minutes over the course of three days. Isner won.

Video Games

1. What name was given to the character who would later become Super Mario when he made his first appearance in the 1981 game *Donkey Kong*?

2. Which video game franchise usually releases its games in pairs, such as *Red* and *Blue*, or *Sword* and *Shield*?

3. The first handheld game console to use interchangeable cartridges was released in 1979 but what was it called?

4. When used in video games, what do the letters HP typically stand for?

5. *The Legend of Zelda* games are set in which magical land?

6. In what year was the first *The Sims* game released?

7. As of 2023, what is the bestselling game console of all time?

8. Master Chief is the central figure in which video game series?

9. The Chocobo is a fictional species of bird from which video game franchise?

10. Which video game features ghosts called Inky, Blinky, Pinky and Clyde?

The original plan for the Nintendo 64 game GoldenEye 007 *was to have Roger Moore, Sean Connery and Timothy Dalton as playable characters. Although this idea was scrapped, their character models still exist in the game.*

Holidays

Christmas

1. The Christmas tree is a tradition that comes from which country?

2. Which children's character had the Christmas number one in 2000?

3. What does my true love give to me on the third day of Christmas?

4. Christmas Island is an external territory of which country?

5. What is the name of the character Will Ferrel plays in the Christmas film *Elf*?

6. Kilted soldiers is another name for which foodstuff, usually present in a Christmas dinner?

7. Which of these people don't appear in the film *Love Actually* – Alan Rickman, Colin Firth, or Kenneth Branagh?

8. The Christmas Truce took place in the trenches of World War I in what year?

9. What is the star sign of someone born on Christmas Day?

10. Although Santa obviously lives at the North Pole, which UK city hosted the world's first Christmas grotto?

Cobwebs and spiders are traditional Christmas tree decorations in Ukraine.

Halloween

1. Which horror film features the iconic line, "They come at night … mostly"?
2. In the 1962 novelty song "Monster Mash", what is the name of the house band that Dracula joins?
3. Who hosts the radio and TV series *Uncanny*, which explores paranormal and supernatural phenomena?
4. The term "zombie" comes from the folklore of which island nation?
5. Which Scottish poet wrote a 1785 poem called "Halloween"?
6. Harry Potter and friends spend their first Halloween at Hogwarts confronting which creature in the girls' bathroom?
7. Sweeny Todd is the demon barber of which location in London?
8. Barmbrack is a type of quick bread containing sultanas and raisins that is popular around Halloween in which country?
9. Ichabod Crane is the main character in which spooky story by Washington Irving?
10. Which country produced the world's first purpose-built haunted attraction in 1915?

The 1982 film Poltergeist *used real skeletons on set as it was cheaper to buy them than make fake ones.*

Holidays

1. On what day of the week is Mardi Gras always held?

2. In the USA, what month is Mother's Day celebrated?

3. Chinese New Year in 2024 will mark the start of the Year of which animal?

4. In Hamlet, which holiday is ruefully mentioned by Ophelia in Act 4?

5. Who is credited with writing the poem "Auld Lang Syne", traditionally sung at New Year celebrations?

6. Oktoberfest is held annually in which German city?

7. Which cake, associated with Lent and Easter, has layers of marzipan and a set of eleven balls on top of it?

8. How many days of Kwanzaa are there?

9. In Switzerland, what creature traditionally delivers Easter eggs?

10. In what month is Canadian Thanksgiving held?

On Good Friday in Bermuda, it is traditional to fly kites on the beach.

Food & Drink

Dessert

1. Eton mess contains strawberries, but what fruit is used in Lancing mess?

2. What was the first flavour of Angel Delight?

3. Traditionally what alcohol is poured on a Christmas pudding before setting it alight?

4. What sort of pastry is used to make eclairs?

5. What two colours are traditionally used for the inside of a Battenberg cake?

6. Which fruit is a hybrid of a pomelo and a mandarin?

7. Which traditional English baked good has a meat, potato and vegetable filling on one end, and a jam filling on the other?

8. How many times are biscotti biscuits baked?

9. In what decade did the first Krispy Kreme store open?

10. What is the name of the Italian dessert that translates to "cooked cream"?

Raspberries, apples, cherries, plums, strawberries and peaches are all from the same family of plants as roses.

Food

1. What fish is traditionally used to make kedgeree?

2. In what decade did McDonalds introduce the Happy Meal?

3. Which cereal brand has three mascots called Snap, Crackle and Pop?

4. What was the first food to be microwaved on purpose?

5. What scale is used to measure the heat of chili peppers?

6. A Whitby bun is flavoured with which fruit?

7. Roquefort cheese is made from the milk of which animal?

8. Lincolnshire sausages are flavoured with which herb?

9. What fruit is the basis of a melba sauce?

10. The original Colin the Caterpillar is a product of which retailer?

In 1834, tomato ketchup was sold as a cure for an upset stomach. It was decades before it gained popularity as a condiment.

Whiskey & Wine

1. The wine region of Marlborough produces almost three quarters of which southern hemisphere country's wine?

2. Mead is an alcoholic drink made from fermenting which ingredient with water?

3. Cava is a sparkling wine from which country?

4. Jack Daniel's, the bestselling whiskey in the world, is produced in which US state?

5. Which wine grape shares its name with the capital city of Oman?

6. What P is the name for the dimple in the bottom of some wine bottles?

7. Which country drinks the most wine per capita?

8. In 2001, which country's single malt won the "Best of the Best" at Whisky Magazine's awards, catapulting its whiskies into the international spotlight for the first time?

9. What is the term for a champagne bottle that contains the equivalent of 35 regular bottles?

10. Which white wine originated in the Rhine region of Germany?

In Ancient Greece, the host of a dinner would take the first sip of wine to reassure the guests that it wasn't poisoned. It's believed this is where the phrase "drinking to one's health" comes from.

World Cuisine

1. Roast lamb, meat pie and pavlova are all national dishes for which nation?

2. The national dish of Jordan, Mansaf, is which meat cooked in fermented, dried yoghurt and served with rice?

3. Lukanka is a type of sausage unique to the cuisine of which European nation?

4. Bra, Bitto and Taleggio are all cheeses with protected geographical status in which country?

5. In Indian cuisine, the word "aloo" means which vegetable will be central to the dish?

6. Which country produces and exports the most olives?

7. Chevon is the term for meat from which animal?

8. In sushi, if you were to order unagi, what can you expect to be served?

9. The name of which Italian food comes from the local word for "thin string"?

10. The German food sauerkraut is made from which vegetable?

Caesar salad has nothing to do with Rome, and was in fact invented in Mexico in 1927.

Miscellaneous

Family & Friends

1. In the sitcom *Friends*, which city do Ross and Emily get married in?

2. The daughter of Chris Martin and Gwyneth Paltrow is named for which fruit?

3. Dunbar's number is a suggested limit of how many stable relationships one is able to maintain – but what number is it?

4. Which musical superstar is the godfather of Romeo and Brooklyn Beckham?

5. What surname is shared by the family members Shirley, Keith, Danny, Chris and Laurie?

6. Which of Henry VIII's wives was the mother of Mary I?

7. What is the name of Will's actor friend in the sitcom *Will & Grace*?

8. George Bush and George W Bush were a father-son duo that both served as US president. What is the surname of the only other father and son to hold the role?

9. Which writer once outstayed his welcome at Charles Dickens's house, causing an irreparable rift in their friendship?

10. Who is the eldest of the Kardashian sisters?

The length of time between the first powered flight and the first moon landing is so small that Buzz Aldrin's father was friends with the Wright Brothers.

General Knowledge

1. Mark Zuckerberg was at what university when he invented Facebook?

2. What was the first manmade thing to break the sound barrier?

3. What rank is shared by the fictional characters Sparrow, Haddock and Smollett?

4. What type of alcohol is made from the blue agave plant?

5. The Mary Celeste was found abandoned in 1872 off the coast of which Atlantic islands?

6. In boxing, what division comes between lightweight and middleweight?

7. What is the only number that is twice the sum of its digits?

8. According to the Good Beer Guide 2020, what is the most common pub name in the UK?

9. What is the only card game that is legally playable in British pubs without requiring local authority permission?

10. What is the name for the first adhesive postage stamp to ever be used in a public postal system?

The only non-human member of the Magic Circle is Sooty.

Houses & Homes

1. Vaduz Castle is the official residence of the monarch of which country?

2. What is the name of the town where Australian soap opera *Home & Away* is set?

3. Who lives at Number One Observatory Circle?

4. Which country house is used for exterior filming of *Downton Abbey*?

5. What colour are the seats in the House of Lords?

6. Which classic novel is set in the estate of Manderley?

7. What is the term for a structural horizontal block that spans the space between two vertical supports, such as over a door?

8. Which fictional family lived at 1313 Mockingbird Lane?

9. Which architect is famous for the Pennsylvania house Fallingwater?

10. Xanadu is the fictional estate of the title character in which film?

On average, when people move house in the UK they move about nine miles.

Language

1. What is the German word for "bird"?

2. What is the most common first letter of a word in English?

3. The words "umbrella", "torso" and "opera" all come to English from which language?

4. What was the first language spoken in space?

5. In Cockney rhyming slang, what body part are your Hampsteads?

6. All nouns in Esperanto end in what letter?

7. Which flower takes its name because it opens in the morning and closes at night?

8. Which word increased in use by 17000% between 2012 and 2013?

9. What is the Romanian word for "son of the devil"?

10. What is the collective noun for a group of larks?

Ambigrams are words that look the same when turned upside down. Examples include "swims", "suns" and "dollop".

LGBTQ+

1. What are the three colours on the bisexual pride flag?

2. What is the name of Alison Bechdel's 2006 graphic novel about growing up queer?

3. Which country had the world's first openly LGBT head of government?

4. A lavender version of which mammal became a symbol of gay pride after being used in an ad campaign to increase visibility of gay people in Boston in the 1970s?

5. Harvey Milk was the first openly gay elected official in Californian history, but in what city was he elected?

6. What term is used to describe people of a third gender by some indigenous North Americans?

7. In which city did the Stonewall Riots occur?

8. Which event did Caitlin Jenner win a gold medal in at the 1976 Olympics?

9. The British TV series *Queer as Folk* was set in which city?

10. Who was the winner of the first series of *Ru Paul's Drag Race UK*?

Homosexual people are more likely to be left-handed than heterosexual people.

Numbers

1. What is the international dialling code for France?

2. A classic chef's hat has how many folds?

3. In *The Hitchhiker's Guide to the Galaxy*, what is the answer to life, the universe and everything?

4. How many hours are there in the title of the 2010 James Franco biographical film?

5. Which number lends itself to the name of the model of Peugeot launched in September 1998?

6. Seven is considered the luckiest number in the West and in Japan, but which number is the luckiest in China, due to the fact it sounds like the Chinese word for "fortune"?

7. In computing, how many bits make up a nibble?

8. How many inches are in a yard?

9. How many different words make up the entire vocabulary of Dr Seuss's book *Green Eggs and Ham*?

10. What is the highest jersey number allowed in the National Hockey League?

Although you can only fold a standard piece of paper seven times, theoretically if you folded it 103 times, its thickness would be the same as that of the observable universe.

Philosophy

1. A statue of which Scottish philosopher sits on Edinburgh's Royal Mile, with local tradition suggesting he has a lucky toe?

2. In Ancient Greece, which philosopher set up the Academy?

3. Which French philosopher is most notable for his statement, "I think, therefore I am"?

4. What S is the philosophical idea that only one's mind is sure to exist?

5. The Asian philosopher Confucius was born in which country?

6. The tomb of which philosopher, found in Highgate Cemetery, is now a Grade I listed structure?

7. Which philosopher was the mother of author Mary Shelley?

8. Which English philosopher wrote the 1651 book *Leviathan*, which expounds on social contact theory?

9. What E is the branch of philosophy that studies knowledge itself?

10. According to the song "What I Am" by Edie Brickell and the New Bohemians, if religion is found in the smile of a dog, where is philosophy found?

Plato once argued that a human was nothing more than a "featherless biped". Diogenes plucked a chicken and handed it to him, so Plato added humans also had "broad, flat nails".

Under & Over

1. In what year did the Disney song "Under the Sea" win the Academy Award for Best Original Song?
2. On the London Underground network, what colour represents the Jubilee line?
3. Which 2006 comedy film features Bruce Willis as a raccoon, Steve Carell as a squirrel, and Wanda Sykes as a skunk?
4. The song "Over the Rainbow" was composed for which classic film?
5. The Styx, the Lethe and the Acheron are all rivers in the Underworld of which belief system?
6. Who wrote the 2009 science fiction novel *Under the Dome*?
7. In what decade was the Forth Bridge, west of Edinburgh, completed?
8. In cricket, a single over consists of how many consecutive legal bowls?
9. Who lives in a pineapple under the sea?
10. The Wombles are notable for being found underground, overground and wombling free, and each of them was named for a geographical feature. Which one was named for a South American river?

The shortest journey on the London Underground is between Leicester Square and Covent Garden, taking about twenty seconds.

Something A Bit Different

[73]

Cryptic

1. Phyllis Pechy was the real name of which chef and restaurant critic, who frequently appeared on television with her husband?

2. In which video game series has instalments called *Valhalla*, *Brotherhood* and *Syndicate*?

3. Which neighbourhood of Washington DC is home to the Federal Reserve, the World Bank, and George Washington University?

4. Which 1954 Alfred Hitchcock film was based on the short story "It Had to be Murder"?

5. Which character in the *Transformers* franchise is based on the European Type 1 Volkswagen Beetle?

6. Which 2013 film is a biopic about the pianist Liberace?

7. Which English football club plays its home games at Emirates Stadium?

8. Leo McKern played which fictional barrister on television from 1978 until 1992?

9. Which Destiny's Child single contains a prominent sample from Stevie Nicks' song "Edge of Seventeen"?

10. What links the previous answers?

Famous codebreaker Alan Turing used to keep his mug chained to a radiator.

Initials

1. What links people with the initials TB, GB, TM, BJ, LT and RS?

2. What links people with the initials NA, BA, PC, EM, JY and HS?

3. What links people with the initials ZP, AM, ER, VW, JW and MO?

4. What links people with the initials JC, JM, RH, CE, SS and AR?

5. What links people with the initials DS, PU, KB, JM, AF and AM?

6. What links people with the initials BO, DT, JB, GW, CC and JA?

7. What links people with the initials MM, NF, KG, LT, SD and DO?

8. What links people with the initials KI, JF, DL, BD, HP and TM?

9. What links people with the initials JA, CC, LK, ML, MP and DS?

10. What links people with the initials LA, BH, JC, TM, CA and EF?

J was the last letter to be added to the English alphabet, coming along around the year 1500.

Odd One Out

1. Goat, Panda, Monkey, Dog

2. Trump, Clinton, Kennedy, Buchanan

3. Mastiff, Beagle, Bulldog, Basenji

4. Bournville, Twirl, Aero, Picnic

5. Mike Todd, Richard Burton, Larry Fortensky, Maxwell Reed

6. Louis, George, Archie, Charlotte

7. Thailand, Mongolia, Nepal, Azerbaijan

8. Claire Foy, Helen Mirren, Imelda Staunton, Olivia Colman

9. Artemis, Helios, Hephaestus, Poseidon

10. Kate Winslet, Hilary Swank, Meryl Streep, Vivien Leigh

Giraffes are the only animals to have horns from birth. The technical term for them is "ossicones".

Sequences

1.   Thrones, Kings, Swords ...?

2.   Slovakia, Eritrea, Palau ...?

3.   F1, B16, JP2 ...?

4.   Garnet, Amethyst, Aquamarine ...?

5.   Snow Leopard, Lion, Mountain Lion ...?

6.   *Everything Everywhere All At Once, CODA, Nomadland* ...?

7.   Bull, Twins, Crab ...?

8.   He, Ne, Ar ...?

9.   Talc, Gypsum, Calcite ...?

10. Euan, Nicholas, Kathryn ...?

Since 1825, the leaders of Russia have alternated between being bald and having hair.

Wikipedia

In this round, each statement comes from a Wikipedia page (at time of writing). Identify which Wikipedia page the line has come from.

1. NOVEL: *The novel is set in Kent and London in the early to mid-19th century and contains some of Dickens's most celebrated scenes, starting in a graveyard, where the young Pip is accosted by the escaped convict Abel Magwitch.*

2. COUNTRY: *Following the death of President Juan Perón in 1974, his widow and vice president, Isabel Perón, ascended to the presidency, before being overthrown in 1976.*

3. MOUNTAIN: *It is the second-most prominent mountain in Europe, after Mount Elbrus, and it is the eleventh most prominent mountain summit in the world.*

4. BIRD: *It builds the largest nest of any North American bird and the largest tree nests ever recorded for any animal species, up to 4 m (13 ft) deep, 2.5 m (8.2 ft) wide, and 1 metric ton (1.1 short tons) in weight.*

5. PRIME MINISTER: *His premiership was dominated by the question of policy towards an increasingly aggressive Germany, and his actions at Munich were widely popular among the British at the time.*

6. BRITISH CITY: *Iron Age hillforts and Roman villas were built near the confluence of the rivers Frome and Avon.*

7. ELEMENT: *[It] has the highest atomic number of any stable element and three of its isotopes are endpoints of major nuclear decay chains of heavier elements.*

8. COCKTAIL: *In the United States, it is usually consumed in the morning or early afternoon, and is popular as a hangover cure.*

9. ACTOR: *[He] is one of the few performers to have achieved what Radio Times calls the "Holy Grail of Nerd-dom", having played popular supporting characters in* Doctor Who *(2005),* Star Trek *as Montgomery "Scotty" Scott (2009–2016), and* Star Wars: The Force Awakens *(2015).*

10. MUSICAL INSTRUMENT: *They can be mounted, for example on a stand as part of a drum kit (and played with drum sticks), or they can be held in the hand and played by tapping, hitting, or shaking the instrument*

The first person to have a Wikipedia page created for them was 18ᵗʰ century Scottish philosopher Thomas Reid.

Answers

Film & Television

Actors

1. *The Godfather*
2. *My Fairy Lady*
3. Hedy Lamarr
4. *Philadelphia* or *Forrest Gump*
5. 2007
6. Kate Winslet
7. Rachel McAdams
8. Aquaman
9. Anya Taylor-Joy
10. Kenneth Branagh

Film

1. Liesl
2. Francisco Scaramanga
3. Rabbit
4. Feather
5. *The Italian Job*
6. *Sleeping Beauty*
7. *Get Out*
8. Carrot
9. *The Incredibles*

10. Spaghetti

Reality Television

1. 2011
2. *Love Island*
3. Davina McCall
4. Teapots
5. Brentwood
6. *The Traitors*
7. Paul Hollywood
8. *The Voice*
9. South Korea
10. *You're Fired*

Science Fiction Films

1. *Dune*
2. Tatooine
3. Xenomorph
4. Arthur C Clarke
5. *The Wrath of Khan*
6. Clara Clayton
7. Sandra Bullock
8. ET
9. *Galaxy Quest*
10. Chris Evans

Sitcoms

1. *Days of our Lives*
2. Button House
3. AFC Richmond
4. *Derry Girls*
5. Olivia Colman
6. Saffron (Saffy)
7. Elizabeth
8. Miranda Richardson
9. Hyacinth Bouquet
10. Greendale

Television

1. *Orange is the New Black*
2. Josh Widdicombe
3. Bouvier
4. Pedro Pascal
5. He breaks his glasses
6. Clive Myrie
7. Pontypandy
8. Alexander Armstrong
9. Wimbledon
10. *Rainbow*

History

[83]

Exploration

1. Vasco da Gama
2. Valentina Tereshkova
3. Africa
4. Australia
5. Pathfinder
6. HMS Resolution
7. Antarctica
8. Z
9. Pacific Ocean
10. 1995

History

1. Elizabeth I
2. Mercia
3. Augustus
4. Cleopatra VII
5. 1605
6. Physics
7. Sydney
8. Whigs
9. 1912

10. Ever Given

Noughties

1. Beijing
2. 2001
3. Serbia
4. Robert Langdon
5. King Charles III and Queen Camilla
6. *Wii Sports*
7. 2009
8. *Shrek 2*
9. Carol Ann Duffy
10. Elephant

Prehistory

1. Bronze Age
2. Eruption of the Toba Volcano
3. Indonesia
4. Skara Brae
5. Alps
6. China
7. Copper
8. Lucy
9. Dog

10. Germany

Stuarts

1. Robert II
2. James II & VII
3. Pudding Lane
4. Ludgate Hill
5. Inigo Jones
6. 1701
7. Cavaliers
8. Lord Protector
9. Torbay
10. Norwich

War

1. Luftwaffe
2. American Civil War
3. Amsterdam
4. Henry V
5. Harold Godwinson
6. Operation Barbarossa
7. China
8. Lance
9. Battle of the Somme

10. Fanta

Science & Nature

Animals

1. Gorilla
2. Buck
3. Polar bear
4. Cretaceous
5. Axolotl
6. Coral
7. Giraffe
8. Skunk
9. Black Beauty
10. Armadillo

Botany

1. Raspberry
2. Dandelion
3. Holly
4. Garlic
5. Cacti
6. Gladiolus
7. Ikebana

8. Foxglove

9. Oak

10. Xylem

Chemistry

1. Nitrogen

2. Oganesson

3. Two

4. Mercury

5. Protons and neutrons

6. Pu

7. Red

8. Sweden

9. Lithium

10. Iodine

Creepy Crawlies

1. Five oranges

2. Beetles

3. Francis

4. Ants

5. Dragonflies

6. Cricket

7. Red

8. *Madama Butterfly*

9. Radula

10. 1930s

Dogs

1. Laika

2. Corgi

3. Janitor

4. Baha Men

5. Japan

6. Old English Sheepdog

7. Cerberus

8. Scottish Terrier

9. Lassie

10. *101 Dalmatians*

Science

1. Fallopian tubes

2. Kidney

3. Blue

4. Vinegar

5. Troposphere

6. Bus

7. Louise Brown

8. Eye

9. Silver and gold

10. Eggs

Space

1. Uranus

2. Apollo 11

3. The presence of water

4. Phobos

5. Mercury

6. Ursa Minor

7. Iron

8. Neptune

9. Neil Armstrong's footprint

10. Charon

People

Daniel(le)

1. Daniel Radcliffe

2. *The X Factor*

3. *Casino Royale*

4. Danielle Steel

5. *Skins*

6. *Phantom Thread*

7. Tracy Beaker

8. Oingo Boingo

9. Psyche or Mirage

10. George H W Bush

George

1. Two

2. George II

3. Yellow

4. Doug Ross

5. Ear

6. George Orwell

7. Walker

8. Six

9. "Careless Whisper"

10. *Seinfeld*

Jo & Joe

1. Delaware

2. Purdey

3. Tom Hanks

4. Henry VI, Part I

5. French Resistance

6. John Whaite
7. Lady Gaga
8. New York Yankees
9. Supernanny
10. Nikita Khrushchev

Mary

1. Todd
2. *The Last Man*
3. 1960s
4. Mary J Blige
5. School
6. Cherry Tree Lane
7. Gabriel
8. Victoria sponge
9. Liz Truss
10. Crimean War

Michael

1. *Bad*
2. Steve Jobs
3. Liverpool
4. *Superbad* or *Juno*
5. *Ripping Yarns*

6. *Wall Street*
7. David Brent
8. Michael Phelps
9. 2003
10. 29th September

Rachel

1. S Club 7
2. Oxford
3. Daphne du Maurier
4. Two
5. Jacob
6. *Waterloo Road*
7. Rod Stewart
8. Rachel Weisz
9. Rachel Maddow
10. Meghan Markle

Music & Theatre

Classical

1. George II
2. Piccolo
3. Ludwig

4. Richard Wagner

5. Piano

6. Jupiter

7. Claude Debussy

8. William Hogarth

9. Chopin

10. Italian

Music

1. The Police

2. David Bowie

3. Songs of Innocence

4. Plan B

5. Jazz

6. Billie Holiday

7. The Comets

8. Sister Rosetta Tharpe

9. Robert Johnson

10. Drums

Musicals

1. *Blood Brothers*

2. *Mamma Mia!*

3. Rodgers & Hammerstein

4. *La Boheme*

5. *Moulin Rouge*

6. *Hadestown*

7. Elphaba

8. "We Don't Talk About Bruno"

9. Contralto

10. *The Producers*

Number Ones

1. "Waterloo"

2. "Here in My Heart"

3. Westlife

4. "(Everything I Do) I Do It For You"

5. Madonna

6. *No Time to Die*

7. Ten

8. Little Jimmy Osmond

9. Zero

10. George Harrison

Theatre

1. Othello

2. John Adams

3. Antoinette Perry

4.   1950s

5.   Kit Marlowe

6.   They all closed on their opening nights

7.   Peacock

8.   Harold Pinter

9.   *Operation Mincemeat*

10. Donkey (Ass)

Art & Literature

Art

1.   Michelangelo

2.   William Shakespeare

3.   Johannes Vermeer

4.   Marc Quinn

5.   Sunflower seeds

6.   Nighthawks

7.   Georgia O'Keeffe

8.   Bed

9.   Claire

10. Frida Kahlo

Books

1. *Dracula*
2. Stuart Turton
3. *The Great Gatsby*
4. Spanish
5. Hercule Poirot
6. Flowers
7. *Diary of a Nobody*
8. *Pride & Prejudice*
9. *Pinocchio*
10. *The Secret History*

Kids Books

1. Wormwood
2. Kansas
3. Aunt Sponge and Aunt Spiker
4. Whoville
5. Mongoose
6. David McKee
7. Triangle
8. Jadis
9. Hedgehog
10. Hundred Acre Woods

Literature

1. Unseen University
2. *One Day*
3. War
4. *Little Women*
5. Miss Havisham
6. Soma
7. Seagull
8. *Wuthering Heights*
9. Khaled Hossieni
10. *Casino Royale*

Statues & Sculptures

1. Peter Pan
2. India
3. Gustave Eiffel
4. Walt Disney and Mickey Mouse
5. Bronze
6. The Fourth Plinth in Trafalgar Square
7. Antony Gormley
8. Millicent Fawcett
9. Florence
10. The Little Mermaid

Religion & Politics

Judaism

1. Glass
2. Lilith
3. Elijah
4. Passover (Pesach)
5. Asheknazi
6. Nine
7. Nisan
8. Tanakh
9. Twelve
10. *Friday Night Dinner*

Kings & Queens

1. Charles II
2. Richard III
3. Mary, Queen of Scots
4. Royal Standard
5. Edward VI
6. Felipe VI
7. 25
8. 1901
9. Napoleon III

10. James Bond

Mythology

1. Bastet

2. Ambrosia

3. Fimbulwinter

4. Jupiter

5. Eight

6. Moon

7. Charon

8. Five

9. Feather

10. Chaos

Politics

1. Spencer Perceval

2. Enda Kenny

3. Khmer Rouge

4. Thirty minutes

5. Rose

6. The worst possible people

7. Tony Blair

8. Betty Boothroyd

9. Paddy Ashdown

10. Egg

Religion

1. Kirpan

2. Ramadan

3. Jehovah's Witnesses

4. Hinduism

5. Four

6. Noah

7. Greece

8. Islam

9. Pelican

10. Wittenberg

World Leaders

1. Franklin D Roosevelt

2. 35

3. Pius XII

4. South Korea

5. Chile

6. Woodrow Wilson

7. Brazil

8. New Zealand

9. The Dalai Lama

10. Gerald Ford

Geography

Asia

1. Indonesia

2. Buddhism

3. Cambodia

4. 1997

5. Japan

6. Kazakhstan

7. Mango

8. Urdu

9. Mekong

10. Seoul

Britain

1. 1966

2. Westward Ho!

3. Glasgow

4. Cumbria

5. Glamorgan

6. St David's

7. Pennines

8. High Street

9. Tamar

10. Bank

Europe

1. Iberian Peninsula

2. Bergen

3. Bonn

4. Greece

5. Sweden

6. Gavrilo Princip

7. Islam

8. 1986

9. Lisbon

10. 1916

Geography

1. Angel Falls

2. Croatia

3. Caldera

4. Wellington

5. USA and Canada

6. Mali

7.   Minnesota

8.   Emergent

9.   Luxembourg

10. Caribbean Sea

Landmarks

1.   Blue

2.   CN Tower

3.   Sydney Opera House

4.   Elizabeth Tower (accept Big Ben)

5.   Moscow

6.   Brussels

7.   Loch Lomond

8.   Stonehenge

9.   Great Wall of China

10. Peru

Mountains

1.   Mount McKinley

2.   China and Nepal

3.   England

4.   South Dakota

5.   Big Rock Candy Mountain

6.   Mount Olympus

7. Andes
8. Mount Doom
9. Mont Blanc
10. Matterhorn

Sport & Games

Athletics

1. Discus
2. Tessa Sanderson
3. Wrestling
4. Three
5. Sixteen
6. Budapest
7. Tanni Grey-Thompson
8. Zola Budd
9. 100 metres
10. High jump

Board Games

1. Atlantic City
2. French
3. Aircraft carrier

4. Yellow

5. Roo

6. King

7. 54

8. Six

9. Purple

10. Five

Football & Rugby

1. Arsenal

2. Thirteen

3. Edinburgh

4. Brighton & Hove Albion

5. Ireland

6. Prop

7. South Africa

8. Uruguay

9. The Canaries

10. Nine

Sport

1. Athens

2. Evander Holyfield

3. Los Angeles Lakers

4. India

5. Red

6. The Undertaker

7. Melbourne

8. Sixty

9. Three

10. Croquet

Video Games

1. Jumpman

2. *Pokémon*

3. Microvision

4. Hit Points

5. Hyrule

6. 2000

7. Playstation 2

8. *Halo*

9. *Final Fantasy*

10. *Pacman*

Holidays

Christmas

1. Germany

2. Bob the Builder

3. French hens

4. Australia

5. Buddy

6. Pigs in blankets

7. Kenneth Branagh

8. 1914

9. Capricorn

10. Liverpool

Halloween

1. *Aliens*

2. Crypt-Kicker Five

3. Danny Robins

4. Haiti

5. Robert Burns

6. Troll

7. Fleet Street

8. Ireland

9. The Legend of Sleepy Hollow

10. England

Holidays

1. Tuesday
2. May
3. Dragon
4. Valentine's Day
5. Robert Burns
6. Munich
7. Simnel cake
8. Seven
9. Cuckoo
10. October

Food & Drink

Dessert

1. Bananas
2. Strawberry
3. Brandy
4. Choux
5. Pink and yellow
6. Orange
7. Bedfordshire Clanger

8. Twice

9. 1930s

10. Panna cotta

Food

1. Haddock

2. 1970s

3. Rice Krispies

4. Popcorn

5. Scoville

6. Lemon

7. Sheep

8. Sage

9. Raspberries

10. Marks & Spencer

Whiskey & Wine

1. New Zealand

2. Honey

3. Spain

4. Tennessee

5. Muscat

6. Punt

7. France

8. Japan

9. Sovereign

10. Riesling

World Cuisine

1. Australia

2. Lamb

3. Bulgaria

4. Italy

5. Potato

6. Spain

7. Goat

8. Freshwater eel

9. Spaghetti

10. Cabbage

Miscellaneous

Family & Friends

1. London

2. Apple

3. 150

4. Elton John

5. Partridge

6. Catherine of Aragon

7. Jack

8. Adams

9. Hans Christian Andersen

10. Kourtney

General Knowledge

1. Harvard

2. Whip

3. Captain

4. Tequila

5. Azores

6. Welterweight

7. 18

8. The Red Lion

9. Cribbage

10. Penny Black

Houses & Homes

1. Liechtenstein

2. Summer Bay

3. Vice President

4. Highclere Castle

5. Red

6. *Rebecca*

7. Lintel

8. The Munsters

9. Frank Lloyd Wright

10. *Citizen Kane*

Language

1. Vogel

2. S

3. Italian

4. Russian

5. Teeth

6. O

7. Daisy

8. Selfie

9. Dracula

10. Exaltation

LGBTQ+

1. Pink, purple and blue

2. *Fun Home*

3. Iceland

4. Rhinoceros

5. San Francisco

6. Two-spirit
7. New York
8. Decathlon
9. Manchester
10. The Vivienne

Numbers

1. 33
2. 100
3. 42
4. 127
5. 206
6. 8
7. 4
8. 36
9. 50
10. 98

Philosophy

1. David Hume
2. Plato
3. Rene Descartes
4. Solipsism

5. China

6. Karl Marx

7. Mary Wollstonecraft

8. Thomas Hobbes

9. Epistemology

10. On a cereal box

Under & Over

1. 1989

2. Grey

3. *Over the Hedge*

4. *The Wizard of Oz*

5. Greek mythology

6. Stephen King

7. 1890s

8. Six

9. Spongebob Squarepants

10. Orinoco

Something A Bit Different

Cryptic

1. <u>Fanny</u> Craddock
2. *Assassin's Creed*
3. Foggy <u>Bottom</u>
4. *Rear Window*
5. *Bum*blebee
6. *Behind the Candelabra*
7. <u>Arse</u>nal
8. Horace <u>Rump</u>ole
9. "<u>Booty</u>licious"
10. They all contain words for the rear end!

Initials

1. Tony Blair, Gordon Brown, Theresa May, Boris Johnson, Liz Truss, and Rishi Sunak are all 21st century UK Prime Ministers
2. Neil Armstrong, Buzz Aldrin, Pete Conrad, Edgar Mitchell, John Young and Harrison Schmitt all walked on the moon
3. Zara Phillips, Andy Murray, Emma Raducanu, Virginia Wade, Jonny Wilkinson and Michael Owen have all won BBC Sports Personality of the Year

4. Jeremy Clarkson, James May, Richard Hammond, Chris Evans, Sabine Schmitz and Angela Rippon have all hosted *Top Gear*

5. David Suchet, Peter Ustinov, Kenneth Branagh, John Malkovich, Albert Finney and Alfred Molina have all played Hercule Poirot on screen

6. Barack Obama, Donald Trump, Joe Biden, George Washington, Calvin Coolidge and John Adams were all US Presidents

7. Mae Martin, Noel Fielding, Kerry Godliman, Liza Tarbuck, Sophie Duker and Dara O'Briain have all won the UK series of *Taskmaster*

8. Kazuo Ishiguro, John Fosse, Doris Lessing, Bob Dylan, Harold Pinter and Toni Morrison are all Nobel laureates in literature

9. Jennifer Aniston, Courtney Cox, Lisa Kudrow, Matt LeBlanc, Matthew Perry and David Schwimmer all had leading roles in *Friends*

10. Louis Armstrong, Billie Holiday, John Coltrane, Thelonius Monk, Cannonball Adderley and Ella Fitzgerald are all jazz musicians

Odd One Out

1. Panda; it is not in the Chinese zodiac

2. Trump; he is a Republican, not a Democrat

3. Basenji; it is not a British breed of dog

4. Aero; it is not a Cadbury product

5. Maxwell Reed; he was not married to Elizabeth Taylor

6. Archie; he is a child of Prince Harry, not Prince William

7. Thailand; it is the only one with a coastline

8. Helen Mirren; she did not play Queen Elizabeth II in *The Crown*

9. Helios; it is the only Roman god, rather than Greek

10. Kate Winslet; she is the only one without two Oscars

Sequences

1. Crows (last words in titles of books in *A Song of Ice and Fire* series)

2. South Sudan (most recently founded countries)

3. JP1 (initials and numbers of popes, going back in time)

4. Diamond (birthstones from January to April)

5. Mavericks (Mac computer operating systems in order of release)

6. *Parasite* (winners of the Academy Award for Best Picture, going back in time)

7. Lion (zodiac symbols in order)

8. Kr (symbols for the noble gases, going down the periodic table)

9. Fluorite (increased hardness of material on the Moh's scale)

10. Leo (children of Tony and Cherie Blair, from oldest to youngest)

Wikipedia

1. *Great Expectations*
2. Argentina
3. Mont Blanc
4. Bald eagle
5. Neville Chamberlain
6. Bristol
7. Lead
8. Bloody Mary
9. Simon Pegg
10. Tambourine